I Believe I Can Fly

SHIKHER DUBEY

NIYOGI
BOOKS

Published by

NIYOGI BOOKS
D-78, Okhla Industrial Area, Phase-I
New Delhi-110 020, India
Tel: 91-11-26816301, 49327000
Fax: 91-11-26810483, 26813830
email: niyogibooks@gmail.com
www.niyogibooks.com

Design: Write Media

ISBN: 978-81-901936-2-7
Year of Publication: 2005
Second Impression: 2012

Printed at: Niyogi Offset Pvt. Ltd., New Delhi, India

To my grandfather
Pandit Awadh Behari Lal Chaudhary
who was my source of inspiration always

Perform your prescribed duty, without being attached to the fruits of activities. One should act as a matter of duty, for by working without attachment one attains the supreme.

Bhagavad Gita

CONTENTS

- This book teaches you how to make your life meaningful and is a real mantra for success.

(Aparna Dixit, Professor,
Biotech, Jawaharlal Nehru University, New Delhi)

- An excellent book with excellent ideas. Follow it, if you want to change your life.

(R.K.S. Bhatia, National Distribution Manager,
Panacea Biotech)

- This book is the key to success for people from all walks of life. Thanks, Shikher.

(Dheeraj Bhardwaj, Assistant Professor,
Computer Science, IIT, Delhi)

- Shikher has discovered the perfect blend of wisdom and practical experience. This book is really thought provoking.

(Salil Kalyanpur, Product Manager,
Pfizer Limited)

FOREWORD

This book is packed with practical examples that have logical support. *I Believe I Can Fly* helps us to discover our own potential. Most of us don't know what we want, much less have a plan to get it without any proper guidance. Our lives are less exciting and less successful than they could be. This book tells us how to achieve success and how to convert our dreams into reality. It is a step-by-step guide to achieve perfection.

Do you think that you are one of those who have attained success? Are you living your dream life, does every day seem like a wonderful opportunity for great experience? If not, then this book has an important message for you. Your success has a direct impact on your happiness. This book very clearly tells you about all the necessary ingredients for success such as attitude, action, motivation, etc.

It is entirely up to you – what kind of life you want to live. You can make your dream life become a reality by applying the knowledge contained within these pages.

ARUN JAITLEY
M.P., Rajya Sabha

PREFACE

The words of the popular song *I Believe I Can Fly*, from the movie *Space Jam*, are playing in my mind as I write on a subject that transcends the world of dreams and takes you to higher levels of reality. This book has been especially written for people who lead an aimless life and are forever confused and distressed. For them, this book will prove to be the light at the end of the tunnel.

I Believe I Can Fly provides a strong base for people striving to achieve success. It helps them to reach out for the skies, using will power and determination. It will teach them to soar like never before.

Keep your goals in mind, work towards achieving them, and then watch them come alive. Here is a book that will make your dreams real. For, if you can see it, then you can do it.

ACKNOWLEDGEMENTS

I Believe I Can Fly would never have been possible without the relentless support of my friend Manoj Joshi whom I admire enormously. In fact, this book owes its origin to many diverse minds. It began in 2001 when I was going through different kinds of self-improvement books. I am deeply indebted to Jolly Mathew, Training Manager, Novartis, for showing me different ways of learning from these books.

There were many writers and thinkers who inspired me. It is these great minds and thinkers who have always shown others the way. I am grateful to them for they showed me that it was possible to believe that you can touch the sky. For the development of the book itself, I am grateful to my elder brother Shobhit for his love and support. My parents were always there for me, as were my dear friends and colleagues, particularly Nishith Pandey and Pradeep Paliwal. I thank them for their encouragement and suggestions.

1

FOLLOW YOUR DREAMS

There is this story of a powerful king, a man of determination and strong will. His ambition led him to capture many kingdoms. One day, he expressed his desire to conquer an island kingdom and sought the advice of his ministers and army chief. They all advised him against a war with the king of the island who had a very strong army. They feared that they would face defeat. But the king had other plans. He led his army in a large number of ships and reached the island. Once there, he ordered the ships to be burnt down. His army realised that the choice was simple – victory or death. After a fierce battle, the king's army finally captured the island.

It was the king's determination to succeed against all odds that won him the day. He believed he could achieve his goals, and he did. Of course, he had the support of his army.

For any company, its employees are its prime assets. The image and success of the company depends on the efficiency of its employees. If we carry out our jobs assuming it to be our own, there is no room for complacency. Many times, it so happens that our efforts bear no results. But if we keep trying and put in our best effort, success is inevitable. We will fail only if we stop trying. To learn to do something and to do it accurately are two different things. We will succeed if we learn to maintain an equilibrium between acquiring knowledge and applying our knowledge to do it.

You must have dreams – dreams that motivate you to reach your goals. The bigger the dreams, the bigger the goals you set for yourselves. This also ensures that you put in your maximum effort to fulfill your dreams. When you know how big your dreams are, you mentally prepare yourself to be strong enough to actualise them. You find ways to make your dreams come true. Dreams work as a means for setting your targets and they provide you the inner strength to achieve them. After you achieve one goal, you get motivated to reach for other goals.

Motivation, enthusiasm and concentration ensure success. When you are on the verge of achieving your goals, it often seems as if your targets are further than you expected and you fail to find ways to reach them. And just when you start giving up, you realise that you are indeed very close to success. Often you find many hurdles on the road to achieving your goals. However, if you are patient enough and strive forward with zeal and enthusiasm, all obstacles just vanish. The more you try to escape from hurdles or wait for them to pass away, the more are the chances that you will fail. It is important that you keep moving ahead, and focus only on fulfilling your goals.

It is also very important to dream because it is through dreams that you get to see glimpses of your future. Things that we cannot see in our real life can be seen through dreams. The bigger your dreams, the greater will be your achievements. Dreams provide direction to achieve our goals. Dreams also provide an insight into the difficulties and problems that we might face in achieving success. They help us to determine our goal, fuel our ambition, and change our lives. Therefore, it is important to understand our dreams, know their purposes, and analyse the mystery of success. Most human achievements begin with a dream. Dreams are the imagination of our future. So it will not be wrong to say that today's dreams make our future. Expanding your dreams will mean expanding yourself as a person entitled to fulfill the dreams. It's a perception among many people that dreams are only imagination and they never come true. That it is almost impossible to live up to your dreams. This is certainly true to some extent. Nothing is going to help your cause by dreaming alone. Your efforts to make your dreams come true are more significant. At the same time, people without dreams are incomplete people.

Dreams provide a positive attitude. If you have the capability to dream big, then failures really don't hold any significance. Dreams have had a vital role to play in the achievements of all successful people. We should never criticise and make fun of others' dreams. It needs courage and determination to dream and fulfill them. Dreams are the projects of their future and, by their efforts, they make their dreams come true. Dreams affect all aspects of our life – our behaviour, our thoughts and our faith. They provide creativity, direction and a positive attitude.

I remember that when I started my career, I used to travel by bus. Then, I had this small dream of owning a car one day. That year, the company I worked for came up with a scheme for its employees that any member who could achieve the annual target of selling one lakh shampoo bottles would be rewarded with a car. Initially, I found the target almost impossible to achieve. But my desire to fulfill my dream engrossed me in my work and pushed me forward. That year, I actually achieved the target. Had I not dreamt, and worked accordingly, I would have never fulfilled my target. Most of us do not have a clue as to what we expect from our lives. When we need something, we dream of acquiring it and then take the necessary action. And if our actions succeed, so do our dreams. We must thus develop in ourselves the capability to look beyond time. You will often come across people who make fun of your dreams and discourage you to live up to them. In situations like these, you should ignore them and just follow your dreams. Some people wait for things to happen while some make them happen. Success rarely comes to people who wait for things to happen while success is inevitable for those who make things happen.

You should forget all your past failures and focus towards the successes coming your way. There is no point in analysing things that have happened. Instead, work on shaping your future. Do not pay attention to things that frustrate and disappoint you, but find ways that can help you in achieving your goals. Once you start imagining about success achieved as a result of things that have brought them about, then you grow accustomed to such success. There is a saying that good decisions and successes are born out of experience and this experience, in turn, is a result of our mistakes and failures. Our dreams are responsible for what we achieve and what we lose.

Once, during my school days, there was a debate and I wanted to participate in it. I was not a good speaker and was scared to speak in front of an audience. There was a week left for the competition to begin. I used to sit alone, close my eyes, and imagine myself speaking in front of the crowd in the competition and securing the first prize. This continued for the whole week and on the eighth day, when I went to the stage and started speaking, I found I was speaking even better than I had in my imagination. And I actually won the first prize. You sometimes tend to share your dreams with others who do not care much about them. These are people who do not dream and therefore make no progress in life.

They are also the ones who demoralise you. But let not such people bother you. You just follow your dreams. The goals achieved easily do not give us much pleasure. But when we struggle to achieve them, the end result always brings us real happiness.

During my college days, I had a friend who was not very good in his studies. But whenever he saw doctors emerge from a nearby medical college, he would say that he would become a doctor one day. We used to laugh at him because he was only an average student. But he really worked hard to fulfill his dream. When we finished college, he was the first to get admission to a medical college. Today he is a successful doctor in America. It was the power of his dreams that has taken him so far.

Most of us have dreams but we fail to recognise their importance. We keep wondering what it would take to make our dreams come true. The solution is simple – believe in your talent and motivate yourself to live up to your dreams. One fine day, all your dreams will come true. The secret of success lies in carrying out your dreams successfully. Our desires, will power, self-confidence and all available resources help us in making our dreams come true.

Dreams not only give direction to your future, but they also present different possibilities which you can further develop. They give you energy and provide reasons to remain happy. Dreams are your most important treasures. Dreams help in becoming what you want to become. Therefore, realise the importance of dreams. Dreams are precious. And do dream big. Believe your dreams give you wings to fly, and you will find yourself soaring.

2

LOOK BEYOND FAILURE

Success has been defined as failure turned inside out. If you learn from your mistakes, you are bound to overcome failure. It is said that you learn to make good decisions from your past experiences and your experiences are a result of your struggle and poor decisions. It is your failures that make you successful.

Success and hard work are interdependent. If you want to achieve success, you must also be ready to work hard. Sometimes, achieving success might take more time than expected. But your hard work is certainly going to pay off and, eventually, you will achieve success. Hard work never goes in vain.

The bigger your dreams, the bigger are your obstacles on the path to achieving success. But there is no need to be afraid of them. You will have to overcome them if you want to succeed. There are some people who tend to curse their luck when they fail to overcome hardships and obstacles on the way to success. But there are others who believe in creating opportunities out of the obstacles they face. They are the ones who really succeed in life.

Take the story of this young man. Born in a poor family, he struggled throughout his life. But he never accepted defeat. He lost eight times in the election and failed more than once in his business ventures. His mother died early. He started his business with loans taken from people. When his business failed, it took him seventeen years to repay the loan. He wanted to marry, but his beloved died. He suffered a nervous breakdown and was bedridden for six months. But with hard work and courage, Dr. Abraham Lincoln went on to become the president of the U.S.A.

There are lots of people in this world who are talented, educated and intelligent. But all of them do not succeed. In order to succeed, they will have to put in dedication and hard work and follow their dreams. Our knowledge and talent are of little use if we cannot employ them in the best possible way. The obstacles and problems that we face make us strong mentally and physically and help us in moving forward. You'll never fail if you know how to learn from your mistakes. You can change your failures into success with the help of your knowledge and talent. If you fall down, you are not considered a failure. It is important that you try and understand how you feel and how you are going to get yourself going. It does not matter how many times you fall, if you can get yourself up every time. Then, you learn not to fall again and start moving ahead. The better you learn from your mistakes and failures, the more you can carry yourself forward. Unsuccessful people usually lose patience early and stop trying to achieve their goals in life.

Many times, we find no results, even after putting in lots of effort. Success does not come to us overnight. But, as we move forward, it starts coming closer to us. However, once we achieve success, we feel that it has come to us overnight. Our failure doesn't mean we will never taste success. Failures come to make us successful. It's the failures that provide direction and teach us to move forward. Correcting failure is success. Whenever we fail, we are very close to success.

When Thomas Alva Edison was a student, his teachers used to complain to his mother that it was very difficult to teach her son. So Edison's mother wanted her son to study at home. But Edison was so talented that he made a laboratory of his own when he was only ten years old. Edison conducted over two thousand experiments till he finally invented the electric bulb. A reporter once asked him how he felt when he failed so many times. He replied that inventing a bulb was a phenomenon that involved two thousand steps.

Besides learning from our mistakes, it is also important to learn to forget our past failures. Or else, they may affect our future results. Failure is a process that usually comes to us before success, in big or small forms. We should never turn back when we get close to achieving success. We always fear what our future holds for us. This fear of our future spoils our present. People who are successful today are afraid of losing their success tomorrow. The more our fears, the more we are likely to face troubles. So it is important that we overcome such fears.

Michael Jordan, one of the greatest basketball heroes of our time, was eliminated from his school's basketball team when his career was just starting to take off. In his career, he missed over nine thousand shots and lost around three hundred matches. Even then, he is considered one of the best basketball players of all times.

When success overshadows your failures, people only see your success, not your failures. Fear doesn't kill anybody. We come across fear many times in our life. The best way to overcome fear is to face it bravely and boldly and you will see that in no time, it vanishes. When a pigeon comes across a cat, it closes its eyes to get the feeling that the cat has gone away. But, unfortunately, it ends up being eaten by the cat. Most of us have the same kind of attitude. Instead of fighting our fears, we try to save ourselves from being exposed to fear. When this happens, fear tightens its grip over us.

Do not let fear become an obstacle on the way to your success. Find a way to get rid of such fears – failures can either construct or destroy you. It really depends upon how you perceive them. Only those who learn to take failures in their stride can succeed.

When Helen Keller was two years old, she lost her eyesight and speech due to brain fever. She was almost paralysed. But her teacher gave her a new life. Not only did he teach Helen to read and write, but he also filled her with confidence. Until Helen turned ten, she could only communicate through sign language. With her efforts and strong will, she learnt to speak by the time she was sixteen years old. Then she got admission in a school from where she graduated. After Helen finished college, she went on to become a lecturer and started writing books. Her books became so popular that more than fifty of them were translated into different languages. Had Helen lost faith and hope during her childhood, she would have never become so successful.

You are sure to succeed if you carry out your task in the best manner and with complete dedication. We all fail somewhere, sometimes. We also make mistakes. If you recollect your past, you'll find that not a day has passed when you have not made any mistake, be it big or small; or when you have not faced any difficulty or defeat. Difficulties are a part of our lives. We must develop this habit of fighting difficulties. There is a way to fight every difficulty. It depends solely upon yourself and how you do it. Try to control your emotions, thoughts and actions. Take your difficulties as your opportunities and keep moving forward. One of the most important aspects of our life is to solve problems. This reflects our efficiency and our desire to succeed. The people who are responsible for your failures are people with a negative approach, those who always try to discourage and let you down.

When Elvis Presley started his career as a singer, he was rejected by a music company after his first recording. But he didn't lose hope. He met his expenses by driving a truck. Elvis never let his dream die. One day, he got an opportunity to record in a local studio. And then, he never looked back. He became one of the most famous singers of the world. Many of his albums have sold millions of copies worldwide.

We worry about the lack of money, education and health. We never think of finding solutions to solve these problems. Thinking about your problems is not going to help your cause. Instead, your problems will only grow. Franklyn D. Roosevelt was struck with polio at the age of thirty-nine. Even then his political life didn't end there. He became the president of the U.S.A. for three terms.

If you really want to achieve success, then you must first stop blaming your luck and waiting for things to happen. When there is life, there will be problems and difficulties. You must learn to live with them. It is better to fail trying to do something new than to sit idly. At least, you'll learn something in the process. When Alexander Graham Bell invented the telephone in 1876, nobody was ready to buy it. When he exhibited his invention to President Rutherford, the president was quite impressed but wondered who would buy it. The first telephone was hence installed in the president's residence.

Do not be afraid of criticism. Have faith in yourself and in your work. Failures are short-lived and teach you to take precautions on the way to success. Learn to solve your problems with ease and without being depressed. Try to understand your problems. Identify them. Then just uproot them. There are two things that must be kept in mind. First, try to know how serious and difficult your problems are. Second, solve these problems the very moment they crop up, or else they will become more difficult later. Every problem originates with a solution with it. If a problem doesn't have a solution with it, it is not a problem.

Dr. Ken Kooper, the father of aerobics, was a very good athlete during his school days. When he was nineteen, he was healthy and fit. But as time passed by, he did not care much about his eating habits and his health. One day, he found it difficult to swim. From that very day, he made up his mind to improve his health and get stronger and better. He took the best care of his diet and exercised regularly. After thirty years, Dr. Kooper remains as fit and healthy as he was when he was nineteen. Dr. Kooper is the same person who brought about the fitness revolution in America in the sixties.

The day you think you don't have the courage to win, you lose the battle. If you are courageous and have the will to fight all odds, you are sure to win. It's quite possible that you might not succeed even after repeated efforts. But you will surely succeed in the end.

In 1940, Chester Carlson came up with an invention. He went to almost twenty companies with this but no one showed any interest. In 1947, after seven years of searching, he came across a small company in New York, that finally bought his invention and the rights of photostat and copy making. That company went on to become what is better known today as Xerox Corporation. And Chester became a success story.

When things go against your will, it becomes very tough to move forward. You feel you've lost and become distressed. This is the time when your patience, energy and power to succeed are tested. If you overcome this test, then it is you who will make things happen according to your will. Everybody remains content and happy during good times. But those who also remain happy during tough times are sure to succeed.

A person's success cannot be measured by his achievements but by the number of failures that he has faced. There is nothing called failure. Some are less successful while some are more successful. But nobody is a failure. Failures are only meted to those who lose the battle before putting up a fight.

You must have fallen a number of times and hurt yourself when you started to learn to ride a bicycle during your childhood. Did those injuries stop you from trying? Remember, success cannot be achieved in the very first attempt. Failure is an important part of achieving success.

In 1952, Edmund Hillary failed to scale Mount Everest in his maiden attempt. After a few days he was asked to share his experiences with a group of mountaineers. He shouted, "Mount Everest you've defeated me this time. Next time, I will defeat you." A year later, Hillary became the first person to hoist a flag on top of Mount Everest.

Our failures make way for our success. We inherit in ourselves a powerful experience. Make your biggest defeat the tool to achieve your biggest victory. In every problem there lies a solution. Keep in mind that there are miracles in life that you can achieve. But first know that it starts inside of you.

3

YOU CAN DO IT

When you make up your mind about achieving something, you will see that the forces of the universe join hands to make it happen. For, if you can see it, you can do it. If you believe in the action and its results, you will soon find that there is really nothing to it.

All the achievements in your life are dependent upon your actions. Without a positive attitude, the right thoughts and meticulous planning, everything is in vain. Our actions are directly related to our results. The faster your actions, the faster you achieve your results.

In the jungle, the deer knows that it will have to run faster than the tiger if it wants to save itself. The tiger too knows that it will have to run faster than the deer to get its prey or else it will die of hunger. So both these animals run. But the one whose action is faster will survive. If your actions are right and on time, you can make any situation favourable. You will also be able to mould every change in life according to your will. Your actions help you achieve your target. Even if success is not achieved, there's nothing to lose. For, you will get some satisfaction that you tried.

Fortune only favours those who believe in action and hard work. All the achievements and successes of life totally depend on your actions. There is no shortcut to success. You must be prepared and put in the maximum effort on the way to achieving success. If you do not meet your target even after applying the right action, it means that your efforts were not enough. It is important for us to expand our way of thinking if we want to move forward. A hesitant mind not only stops you from shifting your target but also creates obstacles.

Many times, your friends and relatives discourage you and ridicule your efforts. But once you achieve success, they will once again seek your company.

Belonging to a middle class family, this boy had only one dream in his mind. He wanted to become a shooter. When he failed in the tenth standard, his parents were very disappointed. Even after he passed his school examination, they worried about his future. Whenever he was asked what he wanted in life, he used to reply that he would become a shooter. And the rest is history. Ace shooter Jaspal Rana has not only won many medals for himself in this sport, but has also done his country proud.

It is important to have a better coordination between our dreams and actions. When this happens, you'll easily identify the problems and difficulties that may come your way and find solutions for them. Use the experiences that you have gained from your earlier mistakes. Do not repeat these mistakes again. Then you'll surely be able to fulfill your dreams easily.

Lots of people dream. But only those whose actions comply to their dreams turn their dreams into reality. Many people don't have an idea how and where to begin to make their dreams come true. They don't have a clue as to what they want to achieve and how they should go about it. To make any dream come true, it is important to have a vision.

Jack Welch, who was the CEO of General Electric for twenty long years, was considered to be one of the most effective CEOs of all times. He had the ability to coordinate his dreams and his actions. He had a clear picture of what he wanted to achieve and he acted accordingly. His vision and his thoughts were transparent and strong. He was of the opinion that anybody could succeed and remain at the top in one's respective field, provided he went about his work with speed, simplicity and confidence.

It is important for you to keep on trying if you want to achieve your goals and make your dreams come true. It is also important to identify those actions that can lead you to achieve better results. Never curse your luck if you fail because this failure is out of a lack of effort on your part. Blaming your luck will not solve your problem.

If you do not apply action and effort to achieve success, it's clear that you'll require to double your efforts later. So it is wise to start early. If you take action or work hard, you'll certainly get results. Your results depend upon the kind of actions you take.

Compare your actions and their results and find out if there are any differences. If there are, find solutions to correct them. Sometimes, when you analyse your achievements and recollect your past actions, you will find a series of mistakes. This can scare you. It will also influence your future successes. But, instead of fearing them, learn from those mistakes and change the results. One night, when Chanakya was passing through a jungle, he took shelter in a hut belonging to a Brahmin family. When he was served rice for dinner, he put his hand on the hot rice and scalded his fingers. His host advised him to begin eating from the side of the plate where the rice would be much cooler. Chanakya learnt an invaluable lesson. So, instead of defeating his main enemy, Chanakya first dealt with his enemy's close associates and he later took on his main enemy.

If you have ambitions and set targets for yourself in your life then all your knowledge and your internal energy flow. No target can be achieved without facing difficulties. These difficulties provide you an opportunity to learn and show you the way to move forward. Set your target and go all out to get it. Then your results will be far better than your labour, hardship and efforts.

Robert Bruce, the king of Scotland, fought many battles to win his kingdom back. But he failed to succeed. One day he was sitting in an old house where he saw a spider trying to climb a wall. Every time the spider climbed up, it fell down. The king thought that the same thing was happening to him. But suddenly the spider managed to climb the wall. This incident inspired the king so much that he decided to fight again to win his kingdom back.

All roads to success seem to be difficult in the beginning. But once you start moving forward they appear easy. We usually try to defend ourselves from our difficulties. This way, they only increase. But once we fight these difficulties, they will vanish. You will surely succeed if you keep moving. The key to success is in continuous and sustained actions.

If you sit by a seashore, you'll find that the waves gradually cause the rocks to erode, even though the rocks are stronger. But the action of the waves is continuous. Even though the waves appear to be weaker than the rocks, they are ultimately more powerful.

Sometimes, we don't act until we think it's time to do so. If actions are carried out at the right time, you have a better chance of success. We can do anything in several attempts, but if we can make it happen in the very first attempt, we save the time required to do it.

During your effort, you'll get a chance, when you can convert your failures into success. Don't let such chances go away.

We can achieve big successes through small efforts. But such successes depend entirely upon our actions. When you truly want to achieve something or do something extraordinary, your age and your resources never create obstacles. You can work wonders if you have faith, patience and fire in your belly.

When General Sunders retired at the age of sixty, he felt that the money he had earned was not enough for a living. He felt a sudden urge to do something extraordinary. He analysed what he was best at and felt that he had an extraordinary recipe to prepare chicken curry, that nobody knew about. In order to sell this recipe, he contacted many restaurants, but without success. Finally, after two years of long search, he came across a restaurateur in Kentucky who took mercy on him and asked him to reveal his recipe. Today Kentucky Fried Chicken is a huge business enterprise and one of the world's most well known brands.

The biggest contributions towards Sunders' success were his continuous effort, self-confidence and patience.

If you fail once, it doesn't mean you stop trying. This is the reason why people fail. After a single failure, they change their target and think of doing something different. Keep on working towards your goals until you finally succeed. It is very important to realise our responsibilities, find our resources, and to find ways to achieve our goals. There are three types of people in this world – there are those who want to become rich, the second group wants to earn fame, and finally there are those who want power. All of them try to fulfill their needs in their own ways.

But there are also some people who want to achieve everything without doing anything. Such people will never be successful. We achieve success as a result of years of dreaming, making sacrifices and working hard.

If you believe in changing your output, make sure that your input is also different. You have to first change yourself because your actions will reflect what you are. Change yourself internally. If you want to achieve anything in your life, you can achieve it.

Not only do your actions bring results, honour and fame, but they also provide you with peace and happiness. When we keep ourselves busy, the capacity of the brain to perform increases. We start to think in a more innovative manner and make the correct decisions. When you achieve success, you get a sense of satisfaction and happiness.

If you are looking for happiness, you will have to work with all your heart. The biggest assets of your life are your thoughts and if they are with you, you can achieve anything that you want.

Besides your personal goals, also think what you can do for others. Your actions should be such that others too benefit from them and derive happiness. If your actions are for the welfare of society, you'll find that you are not alone. Others will help you in the best possible manner. For it is only when you come together, that you can achieve the impossible.

Learn to take responsibility for all your actions. Keep in mind that you alone can shape your life the way you want it. You alone can make it happen. Your actions will determine your future. Never expect others to do your work in order to help you achieve success. Believe you can fly. And you will.

4

SET A TARGET

Positive moves is what it is all about. Life is a game that allows you to play it with your own set of rules. You have to identify your target and then go all out to meet it. But remember you cannot become a good archer if you cannot hit the target. Therefore, it is important to know our targets in life if we want to succeed.

Our targets motivate us to achieve our goals. They are responsible for what we achieve in life. Nothing is possible if we do not set targets for ourselves. Before achieving a bigger target, it is important to set smaller targets and to achieve them. As you start achieving these small targets, you'll soon get closer to achieving the bigger ones. We are quite likely to face a lot of problems and difficulties if we do not set targets for ourselves. For, the target that we set for ourselves works as a key to success.

Mountaineers who scale great heights often succeed because they are filled with self-confidence and know the targets they have set for themselves. They know how many days it would take to scale a height and the difficulties they are likely to come across in their endeavour. They are prepared to overcome all difficulties.

Our goals in life are set by our targets. People without targets have no goals. Such people do not live; they only exist. If you have set targets for yourself, you'll find opportunities all around you. Decision-making is also very important. If we do not have the capacity to make good decisions, our targets will keep on changing with time. To achieve success, it is important to have good decision-making abilities, which help in achieving our targets easily. Most of us feel comfortable and safe walking with the crowd and also set goals and targets in accordance with the crowd. But if you want to create a different identity and become successful, you will have to stand out in the crowd.

When Dronacharya asked his disciples what they could see while aiming at a bird sitting on the branch of a tree, some said that they saw trees, the sky and birds while some saw clouds, leaves and the sky. But when he asked Arjuna, he replied that he could only see the bird's eye. This story from the Mahabharata shows us that when you aim at your target, you must make sure that you do not see anything except the target. We see many things besides our target when we aim for it and thus lose our concentration. This is the main reason for failing to strike our target.

Setting a target is a process that involves concentration and continuity. Our targets keep on changing with our needs and thus we fail to understand what we want to achieve. When we are young, we have a set of dreams for ourselves. As we grow older our dreams and targets change.

Our thoughts get manifested as an image in our mind. We make a mental picture of what we want to achieve. So if we try our best to achieve what we dream of, we can change our whole life. Sadly, there are very few people who work towards meeting their targets. There is only one way that leads to success. You must always know what you want to get out of your life. Wherever you are and however you might be, you must never stop setting targets. It is also important to increase the intensity of your desire to achieve your target.

We all work hard to make our dreams come true. In the race to achieve our target, a few people leave others behind. Some people who do not work that hard reach their target before many who work hard. This is because they know where their targets lie and put in a focussed effort to reach them.

We all see difficulties and problems as obstacles on the route to success. But if we see them as part of the solutions, then we can certainly overcome them. There are no problems to which there are no solutions. Nothing can stop you from winning if you put all your energy, knowledge and talent in fulfilling your target.

It is important to set smaller targets on the way to achieving bigger ones. As we reach the smaller targets, we also come very close to achieving the bigger ones. Achieving the small targets provides us with energy and excitement to conquer the bigger ones. It's like climbing stairs to get to the top. We always begin to climb the staircase from the bottom and then ascend to the top.

In order to move forward, if you wait for conditions to become favourable, you might just end up waiting forever. Nothing can be achieved easily. It requires hard work and struggle. Sometimes, you may find yourself in a situation that troubles you and places hurdles on your way to success. You may find it impossible to reach your target. But with patience and courage, you can change these unfavourable conditions.

Thomas dreamt of spreading his chain of restaurants throughout the country. But he couldn't understand where to begin. He was also in a financial mess. But he was determined to achieve his target. He started with a small restaurant where he also worked himself. At times, he was not able to pay his people. Sometimes he even thought of giving up his dreams, but the desire to achieve his target kept him going. After suffering losses for six months, conditions improved. Today, Thomas' chain of restaurants are spread all over America.

It depends on you how you want to shape your future. Our dreams and targets, our hopes and aspirations make our future. We have to reach our targets in every field of life. This means achieving success in the real sense, be it physical, mental, educational or professional. It is important to maintain a proper coordination between them. Always dream big and set big targets for yourself and make all efforts to achieve them. If you think you can touch the sky, you will soon find yourself spreading your wings and flying there.

5

BELIEVE IN YOURSELF

We usually achieve what we want to. All our decisions and the result of any work are already framed in our mind. And we work according to these. If you feel you can achieve something, however tough it may be, you'll certainly get it. And if you think beforehand that you cannot achieve your target, you'll never be able to achieve it, however easy it may be.

Sri Lanka's explosive opening batsman Sanath Jayasurya was not considered a good batsman when he started his career. When queried about his transformation, he said that somebody in his dreams always told him to punish the bowlers from the very first ball that he faced. He did just that in his dreams and soon went on to do it on the field as well.

We are all born with equal capacities and resources to achieve success. But as we grow up, our capabilities conform into various shapes according to our dreams. Those full of confidence always succeed.

Thomas Alva Edison had this strong desire to succeed since his childhood. In the beginning he conducted many experiments to test his confidence. Once he made bomber wings and tried to fly. He crushed an insect and asked a girl to eat it, and he even sat upon an egg. His mind was full of creative ideas. He wanted to do something new. His confidence led him to success.

Our actions determine the results of our projects. You cannot expect results if you do not act. But if you analyse your results and identify the difference between your dreams and your results and fill the gap between them, you are sure to succeed. Everybody has varied talent. If you do not think big or do not have the desire to achieve something big, all your talents and innovative ideas are wasted.

If you believe in yourself your confidence will work like a light and lead you to the path of success. If your confidence is strong and you still find it difficult to reach your target, God will help you to succeed. For, God only helps those whose confidence levels are high. Not only God, but all the powers of the universe, will help you reach your dreams if your confidence is high enough to achieve success.

During the fierce battle of Mahabharata, Arjuna was on the verge of victory. Then suddenly one of the wheels of his chariot got stuck in a ditch. When Arjuna climbed down to get the wheel out, he just couldn't manage it. Then his charioteer, Krishna, helped pull the wheel out with one hand. Arjuna was astonished to see this. Lord Krishna told him that he lacked confidence in himself and therefore couldn't manage to get the wheel out.

Your confidence always leads you in the right direction. It helps in coordinating between your thoughts and your actions. Lack of confidence in people leads to their failures. Confidence is not only important to your actions, but it also finds importance in your whole life. Your confidence, be it right or wrong, influences your thoughts, mental balance and your decisions.

People do not lack in talent, what they lack is confidence. If you think with confidence what you are going to do before a day starts, you'll find that you'll certainly achieve what you've planned to by the end of the day. You derive confidence from all your actions and your activities and give direction to your confidence and make it stronger. If you dream to succeed, don't let your dream die. Make your confidence high and make your dreams come true.

'If', 'So' and 'But' are words that stand as obstacles between our confidence and our ability to succeed. Our confidence starts getting weaker when we start using such words. The legendary boxer, Mohammad Ali, lacked confidence before two important fights. Before the start of both these matches, he used words such as 'if I win this bout'. And he went on to lose both those games.

Your confidence is made up of what you see, hear and apply. Studying is a very important part of your success, for it helps in strengthening your confidence. The knowledge and experience that you get from studying can help you to gain insights that you can use in your life. Your confidence is strong only when you are determined to achieve your target. If we think more about our results and worry whether they will bear success or failure, we will certainly fail to achieve success. The gap between our capacity to work and the results are due to a low confidence in ourselves. When we lack confidence we say that the work is very tough. However tough your task may be, you can do it if your confidence level is high.

People who train baby elephants tie them with strong and heavy chains. When the elephant tries to free itself and fails to do so, it starts believing that it will never be able to be free. So even when a weak rope is tied to its leg, it doesn't try to free itself. If your confidence gets shaken, there is no point in trying to achieve anything, however great it might be. You can only win if you have the confidence to do so.

To produce and nurture confidence is the same as planting a crop in the field. We sow a seed and then nourish it with fertilisers and irrigate it. In the same way, confidence germinates within you and, to raise it, you'll have to work hard. To keep motivating yourself is also very important. If you succeed in achieving your target and do your scheduled tasks successfully, then nobody needs to encourage you. You will feel encouraged yourself.

Confidence is even more vital than a positive thought. Your confidence determines your thought process. If you are confident, you will make it. Those who fail to achieve their goals tend to blame others. There are very few who accept responsibility and perform their duties.

Always weigh your words and think before you say anything. Develop this habit of talking positively to yourself. This influences your confidence and your thoughts. Always remember that our behaviour and actions are the results of our confidence. Form an image in your brain as to what kind of a person you want to become and then transform this picture into reality by changing your outlook. You'll soon feel the transformation in you. If you want to save yourself from negative thoughts, then avoid the company of people who think negatively.

You'll have to change your style of working and behaviour. If you don't, you'll remain in the same old stage of life where you work in the same old style. If you want to change your life, you'll have to develop a new way of working to achieve success. All the incidents taking place in our life are the results of our thoughts and our actions. Once you stop thinking of words such as possible and impossible, and only look for possibilities, then you'll start looking for differences in results. God's greatest gift to us is our ability to think. And, whatever we think, we can easily turn into reality. Your brain not only helps you to achieve your results in a positive manner but also makes your confidence stronger.

Our brain is divided into two parts – one part helps you to think, survey and analyse. This part of the brain has the capacity to accept or refuse what you have learnt. But we learn most from the other part of the brain, which is as important as the first. Whatever you see, smell or touch becomes a part of your brain. This part of the brain keeps on working and stores everything without analysing.

A friend of mine was inflicted with polio, but that did not deter him from learning about computers and opening a cyber cafe. His confidence and the will to make it big motivated him.

When a massive earthquake shook Gujarat in 2001, a school building in Bhuj collapsed, killing many children. A father reached there to look for his son. He felt that his child was alive and for two days he looked for him under the debris. Many people tried to stop him from doing so, but he wanted to test his faith and confidence in himself. He kept digging and suddenly he heard his child's frantic shout for help. He thus saved his child. It is important to have belief in yourself. Don't let your confidence be affected by others. If you do not have confidence in yourself nobody will have confidence in you.

If you want to change something you must first change your level of confidence. Your confidence can either support or destroy you. Once you are able to change your negative thoughts into positive ones, then you'll be able to change anything in life.

A friend of mine inherited a business from his father. But, since childhood, he wanted to become an I.A.S. officer. He had confidence in himself. He gave up his family business and started preparing for the I.A.S. exams. His family had to face a lot of problems since he was the only working member. He failed twice in the exams, but he did not lose confidence in himself. And finally he cleared the exams in his third attempt and went on to become a successful I.A.S. officer.

You can achieve anything in life if you have confidence in yourself. It is as simple as that. If you believe you can – you certainly can.

6

THINK POSITIVE

Everybody needs to be motivated. For if you believe you can fly, you can. Motivation provides us with the requisite energy to double our efforts towards achieving success. You get motivated in various forms and for various reasons. Success becomes a habit to those who succeed because they don't want to lose this heady feeling. You can learn and get motivated from the success and failure of others and correct your own mistakes. You can also learn the secret of success from successful people.

Jay Endel and Rich De Vose started a company in the city of Washington that dealt in direct marketing. When these two friends started their business, they used to hold sales meetings. For their first sales meeting, they booked a hall for two hundred people. When they started the meeting, there were only two people in the hall. This did not demoralise them. They had two choices – either to abandon their business or to carry on with their dreams. They chose to achieve their dreams and worked according to their target. Today, their company is one of the most reputed and respected companies in the world. Amway International, established in 1959, is now operating around the world.

There is no shortcut to success. The path to success is long, arduous and full of hurdles. But this certainly does not mean that we leave the path due to the fear of such hurdles coming our way. If you want to taste success, these hurdles will only motivate you further. Once you achieve success, it becomes a habit with you. One success will motivate you to achieve another. There was a time when running a mile in a minute was considered to be impossible. No athlete had been able to do so. But Roger Bannister took it as a challenge and ran a mile in a minute. After his stint, nearly five hundred runners have broken this record.

Motivation is a factor which helps you to strike big targets and motivate others to follow you. But you first have to find out which factors motivate others. When you're working in a team to achieve a common objective, it is important to motivate each other equally. If you come to know what motivates a person, then you can easily motivate him to work according to your will.

People's motivational factors vary according to their needs. Some get motivated by money while others get motivated by food, power and so on. Success is the biggest motivational factor. Successful people often get motivated by their internal energy to achieve success. Everybody feels the need for motivation in their lives. Everyone feels the urge to get motivated, but due to prevailing conditions and other factors, the motivation level gets weaker.

Sometimes, unfavourable conditions also motivate people. In 1962, a band of four musicians gave their first audition at Decca Recordings. The managers of the company were not impressed by their music and one of them even went to the extent of saying that he had never heard such music before. This band of four singers went on to become famous world over by the name of The Beatles. Their motivation and self-confidence helped them to reach the top of their careers. In 1944, Emlyn Snowly, director of a leading modelling agency, asked an aspiring model to get a secretarial job or get married rather than become a model. That very model went on to become famous by the name of Marlyn Monroe.

If you get motivated by your smaller achievements you find less difficulties and problems on the way to achieving bigger successes. Motivation is a process that helps you to make your present lively and cheerful by helping you forget your past in the hope of a better future. You are sure to face difficulties and problems on the way to achieving success. But then you will have to remain focussed and motivated to get there.

Wilma Rudolph suffered pneumonia twice in her childhood. When she was four, polio struck her. It was felt that she would never be able to walk again. But with the support of her family and doctors, she began walking with the help of artificial limbs. By the time she was eleven, she removed her artificial limb and learnt to walk normally. Then, she felt that she could even run. She often left school to practice running. Finally, her efforts got results and she was selected for the 1956 para-Olympic team at the age of sixteen, where she won a bronze medal. She also got selected to represent her country again in the 1960 para-Olympic Games. There she won three gold medals in the 100-metre, 200-metre and 400-metre race events.

If you keep worrying all the time, you'll never feel motivated. We often worry about what would happen if we fail. We often fail to motivate ourselves when we worry about how others would react if we fail to achieve success. Such negative thoughts and worries prevent us from getting motivated. So we should never let such worries appear in our minds at any time.

Self-motivation is an essential element in today's fast and competitive life. It helps you to achieve success in anything you do. If you have faith in yourself, you can work wonders. If you are an optimist and believe in positive thinking, it will give birth to motivation in you. If you are an optimist, you'll certainly have dreams; then you'll start motivating yourself to make your dreams come true. All difficult tasks in this world have been done by highly motivated people. They keep moving forward in life continuously and prove themselves successful.

Dhirubhai Ambani, the founder of the Reliance Group, was born in a middle class family in Gujarat. After completing matriculation, he came to Mumbai where he worked as an agent for a cloth manufacturer. He went abroad for a while where he left his clerical job and later returned to Mumbai. There he opened a company with a small capital. Owing to his motivation, self-confidence and vision, today Reliance is one of India's leading business houses.

If you put your negative thoughts aside, you'll find yourself motivated. Spend most of your time with people with whom you feel happy and comfortable. Try to gain and learn good habits from them. Also share your problems and weaknesses with them. Always aim for something different. Develop the habit of remaining happy in life and keep yourself motivated at all times. Meet as many people as you can and develop healthy relationships with them. Also remember to motivate others. Success is like a long journey. You'll have to face a lot of difficulties in this journey. It requires energy to reach your destination. You derive this energy from the love and support of others.

All unique results and achievements are related to motivation. Therefore, it is important to understand as to how much your results are influenced by motivation. People usually get the best result for tasks for which they have been highly motivated. If our morale is low, it affects our capabilities. Motivation is like a battery. If we do not charge it, it stops functioning. So if you want to achieve success, you must have your motivation levels high.

You must also develop the habit of reading inspirational books if you want to get motivated. Good books are like teachers that teach you moral lessons and get you motivated. Good books always show the right path. They are our true friends. So, it is important to develop this habit of reading. We can learn a lot from the achievements of successful people. You can also learn to correct your mistakes. Reading good books can help you to achieve success. Always try to be in an environment of good and successful people. Seek advice from such people because they will be able to show you the path to success and make you aware of the difficulties and problems you are likely to face on this path.

If you come across great people and query them about their aims in life, you are likely to get a very different answer from each. This is what makes them great. When Mahatma Gandhi was once asked to talk about his ambition, he said that he wanted to spread peace and well-being among people and uplift society. Spend your time reading good books and listening to the words of great people.

There is negative as well as positive motivation inside us. My grandfather used to tell me a story of a villager who had two sons. The younger son was well educated and occupied a high post while the other was illiterate. When somebody asked the older son why he had not studied, he said that nobody in his family was educated and so he didn't want an education. When asked the same question, the younger son replied that he wanted to get educated because nobody in his family was educated.

There was a young cricketer who could not display his batting talent because he was sent to bat down the order at the eighth or ninth position. During one of the matches when the team was likely to suffer defeat while chasing a huge target, the captain of the team promoted this player to bat at the fourth position. The young man scored a century and led his team to victory. When asked how he performed this miracle, he said that he got motivated by the responsibility given to him by his captain and the faith that the team had in him.

It hardly matters what you want to do, how and when you want to do. It is quite possible that others might have done what you want to. Then you can know the secret of success from such people and then achieve success in a more effective manner. Sam Bolton, one of the richest persons in America, is famous for doing new and extraordinary things. He went on to become the biggest retailers of all times. He was known for his leadership qualities and the culture he maintained in his company. When asked about the secret of his success, Sam said that it was his capacity to recruit good people and get the best out of them that made him what he was.

Self-motivation is one of the most important aspects of our life. Unless you are self-motivated, you cannot motivate others. You cannot scold or threaten somebody to do something. If you even manage to do so you won't get good results, which otherwise can be obtained by motivating them. Once a child was hitting a tortoise with a stick to force itself out of its shell. When his father saw this, he asked his son not to do so and took the tortoise home. When he placed the tortoise near the fire, it came out of its shell and started crawling. Then he told his son that it was the same in the case of humans. If you force somebody to do something, he will never comply with you. But if you apply the heat of motivation on him, he will be ready to do anything for you.

Many times, we get ourselves entangled in our problems. Instead of solving these problems, we start running away from them. This only increases them. Instead of running away from them, we ought to face them and chase them away. If we are strong and full of self-confidence, no problems and difficulties can trouble us. Derive this self-confidence from motivation.

Good attitude is one of the most important ingredients required to achieve success. Nobody can achieve success without having a good attitude. A positive attitude makes the way to success simple and easy. We set goals and the way to achieve them ourselves. We display our attitude with the help of our viewpoint. The margin between victory and defeat in any game is very little. A positive attitude determines the type of success you want to achieve, in your mind. Sachin Tendulkar plays all his shots in his mind before batting. The wealth, fame and respect that we achieve in life are the results of our positive attitude.

In 1938, a student realised his talent to invent piston rings and sold it to Toyota Motors. He made a small workshop and started working day and night. Due to a shortage of money he even mortgaged his wife's jewellery. And then one day, he finally came up with his invention and exhibited it to Toyota Motors. Unfortunately, the new product was rejected as it did not meet the Toyota standards. He then went back to school for two more years where his teachers and mates poked fun at him. But after facing so many problems and difficulties, he finally achieved success. After two years, Toyota Motors offered him a contract.

When Japan was preparing for war, the Japanese government refused to offer concrete for the construction of a factory to an aspiring entrepreneur. His factory was destroyed a number of times during the war. It was also once badly hit by an earthquake. Soichiro Honda, who didn't know how to ride a car and who rode his bicycle with a motor fitted to it, went on to invent the motor cycle. Today Honda Corporation is a world-renowned company and has over one lakh employees.

You can change your fate and future by changing your attitude. By bringing changes in your attitude, not only do you manage to change your future, but you also make your present stronger. Your attitude has a very huge impact on your life. If your attitude can take you to heights, it can also bring about your downfall.

Your degrees or your birthplace or even your income are not the criteria required to have a good attitude. In your life there will be situations when you find the going tough. But with a positive attitude you can overcome such circumstances and win. The small distance between success and failure can be bridged with the help of your attitude and change your failures to success. Indeed, a positive attitude changes your life. It fills your life with happiness and provides you with satisfaction. If your attitude is good, nobody can stop you from winning. No obstacle can stand up against your attitude. Always keep yourself motivated because it is only you who can motivate yourself. Never stop yourself on the way to success in any situation and never change your attitude.

There was a boy who was very pessimistic in his thoughts. One day his father asked him to leave for the airport by car. He felt his car might break down or he might meet with an accident on the way to the airport and probably miss his flight. So he left for the airport by bus. Unfortunately, the bus on which he was travelling broke down. So he couldn't get to the airport in time and missed his flight.

The more we run away from our difficulties, the more they trouble us. We must fight all odds that come our way with the help of a positive attitude. We usually get lost in our problems, instead of finding solutions to these problems. Make yourself strong enough not to get bogged down by difficulties. If you can fill your brain with images of a bright future, you'll find it easy to fight your difficulties. You'll certainly win then because your dreams for a better future will motivate you and provide you the energy to fight.

A positive attitude will always bring happiness, love, respect, excitement and pride. A negative attitude results in rage, fear, envy, hatred and so on.

There sat a sage on the bank of a river. He saw a scorpion trying to come out of the water. The scorpion tried to come out many times, but every time it slipped back into the water. So the sage took mercy upon the scorpion and tried to get it out of the water. Everytime the sage put his hand on the scorpion, it stung the sage's hand. A man who saw all this asked the sage why he was helping the scorpion out of the water even after it had stung him so many times. The sage replied that it was the nature of the scorpion to sting and it was his nature to save it.

In most cases, success depends upon your attitude towards the incidents occurring in life. If you perceive them in a positive manner, and adopt a positive attitude, you are sure to succeed. All small decisions in your life can bring about a big change. You must be very cautious while making these small decisions. We can take better decisions with the help of a positive attitude. If we bring about a small positive change in our attitude, it will then bring about a big change in our life. If your attitude is positive, you won't get troubled even during bad times. Moreover, you remain happy in unfavourable situations.

If you have two friends, one very optimistic and positive while the other pessimistic and negative, you'll obviously feel like spending most of your time with the former because you'll remain happy and feel motivated with him.

An elderly couple landed in Boston and went to meet the director of Harvard University. After a long wait, they met the director and told him that their son used to study at Harvard but he passed away a year ago. So they wanted to build something at Harvard in the memory of their son. The director felt that they wanted to install their son's statue in the campus so he declined the couple's request. To this the couple said that they did not want to install their son's statue but wanted to donate something for constructing a building. Looking at the couple's ordinary looks and even their ordinary attire, the director haughtily said that it took over seven-and-a-half billion dollars to construct the Harvard University building. To this, the lady looked at her husband and told him that if one can build a university with seven or eight billion dollars, why don't they build a university instead of just a building. So, the Stanford couple established the Stanford University in memory of their son.

Analyse yourself and find out where you think and talk negative. Start your day with excitement. Always remain positive and active. Fill yourself with self-confidence. After you bring about changes in yourself, you are sure to succeed. Keep in mind that once you stop following your target and dreams, then failures will start following you. We all want to achieve something in our lives. Everybody has a dream. According to their dreams, some people strive for money, some for power and fame and there are a few who strive for all of these. But we often fail to understand what efforts are required to achieve them. Usually, successful people declare their aims and ambitions much before they strive to achieve them. It is their self-confidence and positive attitude that help them in achieving success. It is our self-confidence, capabilities and positive attitude that help in making our dreams come true.

It is important to plan how you fight your difficulties and how you react to your problems. Difficulties and problems arise in everybody's lives. But your success will entirely depend on how you get yourself out of the hard times. We often have a limited outlook. But we can change it according to the changes in our conditions. Nobody can change you besides yourself. You can reduce your sorrows, your worries and problems to a great extent with the help of your positive attitude.

In the Seattle para-Olympics, there were physically and mentally challenged sprinters competing in the 100-metre race event. When the race started, one of the sprinters fell on the ground and started to cry. When the other sprinters heard him, they stopped, raised him up and all of them started running together, hand-in-hand. After the race was over the whole stadium gave them a standing ovation.

If something unusual happens, it also goes on to affect your success. Such situations or times don't remain for long. When such unusual incidents vanish, a person gets back to his usual self. If you have a strong base, no sudden changes or incidents can shake it. Set yourself a routine and work according to it. Always be ready to work with a new plan if your previous plan turns out to be a failure. Always try to focus your energies on solving your problems and looking for other available options. We all face difficulties and problems in life and encounter many ups and downs. We might not be able to change our hard times, but we can certainly change ourselves.

We can use all our negative energies into doing something constructive. If we can do this, we will never feel depressed. Never blame anybody for your mistakes. Committing a mistake is no crime. Whenever we try to do something new, we take chances and we are quite likely to make mistakes. We must learn from our first mistake itself. It is foolish to repeat mistakes. It is also not wise to abandon the way to success, fearing our mistakes. Successful people are also human beings like us, after all. Thomas Alva Edison conducted hundreds of experiments and failed many many times before he finally achieved success. Had Edison worried about his mistakes and left his target unachieved, we all might have been living in darkness now. Successful people are those who turn their unfavourable situations into favourable ones.

We must make ourselves strong enough not to get influenced by people with negative attitudes. If you want to correct anything, first, you correct yourself and all things get corrected themselves. People with a positive attitude always aim for big achievements and successes.

A cricket coach was given the responsibility of training two junior cricket teams, X and Y. He had been told that team X had talented and experienced players, while team Y didn't have too many good players. After three months of rigorous training, team X performed comparatively better than team Y. But the truth was that not even team X had good players. The reasons for the success of team X lay in the coach's attitude towards both the teams.

England's economic condition had been badly hit during World War II. In order to avoid further losses, a company shut its manufacturing units one after the other. When the company called for a meeting of its employees to discuss further units being closed, a manager of the company said that it would be better to shut down all the factories at a time instead of shutting one after the other. He went on to ask why no one was seeking solutions to keep the factories open, rather than closing them in quick succession.

Always maintain a balance within yourself. Act with patience and never let your dreams fade away. If we fail once, we tend to change our target very quickly. Don't let this happen. If you want to achieve success, keep moving and follow your dreams. If you have a strong and positive attitude, you'll surely achieve your goals. A positive attitude is the first step on the path to success. It helps in fulfilling your desires and makes your dreams come true. Recite to yourself these powerful words:

I believe I can soar
I see me running through that open door
I believe I can fly, I believe I can fly, I believe I can fly
If I just spread my wings
I can fly, I can fly, I can fly
If I just spread my wings
I can fly